Leonardo DA VINCI

Leonardo DA VINCI

Gareth Stevens Publishing
A WORLD ALMANAC EDUCATION GROUP COMPANY

Please visit our web site at:
www.worldalmanaclibrary.com
For a free color catalog describing World Almanac®
Library's list of high-quality books and multimedia
programs, call 1-800-848-2928 (USA) or 1-800-387-3178
(Canada). World Almanac® Library's fax: (414) 332-3567.

Library of Congress Cataloging-in-Publication Data available upon request
from publisher. Fax (414) 336-0157 for the attention of the Publishing
Records Department.

ISBN 0-8368-5599-X (lib. bdg.)
ISBN 0-8368-5604-X (softcover)

This North American edition first published in 2004 by
World Almanac® Library
330 West Olive Street, Suite 100
Milwaukee, WI 53212 USA

The series "The Lives of the Artists"
was created and produced by McRae Books Srl
Borgo Santa Croce, 8 – Florence (Italy)
info@mcraebooks.com
Publishers: Anne McRae and Marco Nardi

Project Editor: Loredana Agosta
Art History consultant: Roberto Carvalho de Magalhães
Text: Antony Mason
Illustrations: Studio Stalio (Alessandro Cantucci,
Fabiano Fabbrucci, Andrea Morandi)
Graphic Design: Marco Nardi
Picture Research: Claire Andrews
Layout: Studio Yotto
World Almanac® Library editor: JoAnn Early Macken
World Almanac® Library art direction: Tammy Gruenewald

Acknowledgments
All efforts have been made to obtain and provide compensation for the
copyright to the photographs and artworks in this book in accordance
with legal provisions. Persons who may nevertheless still have claims
are requested to contact the copyright owners.

t=top; tl=top left; tc=top center; tr=top right; c=center; cl=center left;
cr= center right; b=bottom; bl=bottom left; bc=bottom center;
br=bottom right

The Publishers would like to thank the following archives who have
authorized the reproduction of the works in this book:
The Bridgeman Art Library, London / Farabola Foto, Milano: 3, 5, 6cl; 8–9,
9t, 12bl, 13, 14bl, 15t, 15cr, 17c, 18, 21t, 21b, 22–23, 26–27, 27t, 28cr, 32, 33t,
34bl, 35bl, 37tr, 41bl, 44bl; Foto Scala, Florence: cover, 4, 11cl, 11b, 15b,
17bl, 17br, 19, 27cr, 31t, 34br, 36cr, 37bl, 43t, 45tr; Corbis/Contrasto, Milano:
Erich Lessing 25b, 45br, Bettmann 7cl, 31b, 39b, Archivio Iconografico,
S.A. 42bl; ©RMN — Michèle Bellot: 35t, 37cl; The Image Works: 44c

The Publishers would like to thank the following museums and
institutions who have authorized the reproduction of the works in this
book: British Library: 29br; © 2003 Board of Trustees, National Gallery
of Art, Washington: 7t; The Royal Collection © 2003, Her Majesty Queen
Elizabeth II: 25cr, 36cl, 38bl, 39cr, 41cr, 43br; Biblioteca Nacional,
Madrid: 30bl

Printed in China

1 2 3 4 5 6 7 8 9 08 07 06 05 04

cover: *The Lady with the Ermine*, **Czartoryski, Cracow**

above: *The Ideal City* (anonymous), **Ducal Palace, Urbino**

opposite: *Self-Portrait* (detail), **Biblioteca Nazionale, Turin**

previous page: *Vitruvian Man*, **Gallerie dell'Accademia, Venice**

Table of Contents

Introduction

Leonardo da Vinci was one of the greatest artists of all time. He was celebrated as a great artist — both painter and sculptor — even in his own lifetime. He was also known as an engineer and a scientist, but the true originality of his work in this field remained hidden for many centuries. With tireless energy, he put his mind to solving a whole range of problems and drew sketches and plans for a host of inventions centuries before they were actually made.

Leonardo's ITALY

Milan · Venice · Mantua · Florence · Rome

▲ *This drawing of an old man, made by Leonardo in about 1513, is believed to be a self-portrait.*

▼ The Holy Family with St. Giovannino *(1456), by Michelangelo, shows the new sculptural quality of Renaissance painting.*

The Renaissance

Leonardo lived during an exciting period in history for art, architecture, and scholarship. It was later called the Renaissance, meaning rebirth, because it seemed that European civilization had been reborn with new ideas. Beginning in the fourteenth century, much of the inspiration for the Renaissance came from the rediscovery of the ancient civilizations of the Romans and Greeks. The great Renaissance artists, such as Leonardo and Michelangelo (1475–1564), tried to match and improve on the impressive skills of the ancient sculptors, and they applied the same energy to making painting more polished and more lifelike.

Leonardo the Man

The Renaissance began in Italy. Its most important center was the city of Florence, where Leonardo trained as a young man. Like all young artists of the day, he learned not only the skills of painting and sculpture but also architecture and engineering. The Renaissance was driven by an energetic spirit of inquiry and the desire to know more and more about the world. Leonardo was also driven by this energy and tirelessly pursued his studies of a vast range of subjects. He was methodical, persistent, and stubborn. He set himself such ambitious tasks that he repeatedly failed to complete them.

Leonardo the Artist

From an early age, Leonardo showed unusual skills as an artist. He had a great belief in the importance of close observation. He noticed, for example, how the shadows around shapes merge softly into one another through gentle gradations of color. He reproduced this in a technique called *sfumato* (from the Italian word for smoke). He also studied the way colors in a landscape lighten and turn to blue towards the horizon, and he reproduced this effect using a technique that he called aerial perspective. His skills as an artist led the way toward much more lifelike art. He believed that artists have special powers of observation and have the skills to translate what they see into images that the rest of the world can understand. Art, he believed, could lead to a perfect understanding of the world. Although Leonardo was also an engineer and a scientist, he believed that his skills as an artist were the most important.

► *Leonardo's portrait of* Ginevra de' Benci *(c. 1474) shows both his sfumato technique of shading and aerial perspective in the background.*

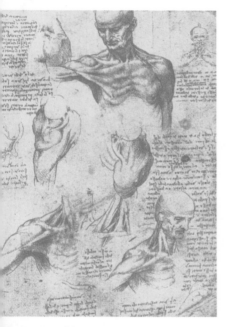

▲ Studies of Arms, Hands, and Feet *(1508–10). Leonardo developed techniques of anatomical drawing that were way ahead of their time.*

► *Most of Leonardo's theoretical and scientific work went unnoticed because it was not published until long after his death. His* Treatise on Painting *was first published in 1651.*

Leonardo the Scientist

His quest for knowledge led Leonardo away from his painting — often to the deep frustration of his patrons, who were paying him to make paintings. By observing, studying, and drawing, he felt he could unveil the secret of life. He filled thousands of pages of paper with drawings and notes about his observations on anatomy, aerodynamics, geology, and optics. Some of these had a direct relevance to painting: he wanted, for example, to see the structures that lay beneath human bodies and the bodies of animals. He was also fascinated with mechanics and how things worked. He used this knowledge for his practical engineering projects, but he also concluded that there was a logical, mechanical explanation for everything in nature.

Leonardo the Inventor

Leonardo used his powers of observation to apply fresh approaches to problems. He toyed with a broad range of ideas way before their time, such as mechanical looms, the airplane, the parachute, tanks, and underwater equipment. These ideas were not developed any further in his day, mainly because they required later developments. Only after they had been invented centuries later did people look back at Leonardo's work and realize that he had been working along the same lines.

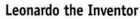

▲ *A model of Leonardo's "auto-mobile," based on a sketch drawn in about 1478–80.*

Young Leonardo

1452 Leonardo is born in or near Vinci, near Florence, on April 15. He lives in his father's household in Vinci. His mother soon marries another man and moves to a neighboring village.
c. 1468 Leonardo moves to Florence, where his father has a successful practice as a notary.
c. 1469 At about seventeen, Leonardo begins work as an apprentice at Verrocchio's workshop in Florence.
c. 1472 He completes his apprenticeship and joins the artists' guild, the Compagnia di San Luca.
1473 He produces his earliest dated work, a landscape drawing. At about this time, he also paints an angel, Christ, and part of the landscape in Verrocchio's *Baptism of Christ* and works on the *Annunciation*.

Leonardo was born in 1452 in a village close to the small town of Vinci, near Florence. His father was Ser Piero di Antonio da Vinci, a young man of twenty-five who came from a wealthy and distinguished family of notaries. Leonardo's mother, Caterina, was a young peasant woman. Ser Piero and Caterina were not married, but Leonardo was welcomed into the family, and his birth was celebrated publicly. Caterina soon married a lime burner, moved to a neighboring village, and had five more children. His father married four times and had eleven more children.

Verrocchio's Workshop

Andrea del Verrocchio (c. 1435–88) was a multitalented sculptor, painter, and goldsmith, and his workshop was considered to be the best in Florence. At the time, artists were rather like craftsmen: they received orders for works of all kinds — painting, sculpture, architecture, jewelry, designs for tapestry, costumes, and theater sets — anything, really, in which design was used. They worked in teams to produce the goods. Among the helpers were young artists who received their training from the master of the workshop.

▼ *Although he had already become an independent artist, Leonardo continued to work for a few years at Verrocchio's workshop. During this time, the* Annunciation *(c. 1473) was created. It shows the moment when the Angel Gabriel tells the Virgin Mary that she will give birth to the son of God.*

Growing up in Vinci

Leonardo received a good basic education in his father's household, but he probably also learned a great deal from his surroundings. He would have seen rich collections of paintings and sculpture in the churches. His interest in mechanics may have been inspired by the technology of the local watermills, potteries, and workshops. In about 1469, at about age seventeen, he began work as an apprentice in the workshop of Andrea del Verrocchio in Florence.

▼ *Vinci as it is today, dominated by the church of Santa Croce and the tower of its medieval fortress.*

Apprenticeship

In Verrocchio's workshop, Leonardo would have been taught all the basic art techniques: how to draw, how to mix and apply paints, how to make clay models for sculpture, and how to carve stone and cast bronze for statues. He would also have practiced life drawing from living models and learned basic anatomy (to help in painting and sculpture), mathematics and geometry, perspective, and engineering — because artists were expected also to be able to design buildings and make practical things such as cannons and canals. In addition, Leonardo may also have learned music in Verrocchio's workshop.

▶ *According to legend, Verrocchio was so impressed by Leonardo's angel, he abandoned color painting.*

▲ The Baptism of Christ (c. 1475–78) was painted in Verrocchio's workshop. It is thought that Leonardo painted the angel on the far left, Christ, and some of the landscape.

▶ The Flemish painter Jan van Eyck (c. 1389–1441) created this work, Man in a Red Turban (Self-Portrait) in 1433. He was one of the first masters of oil painting. He worked in Bruges, Belgium.

Oil Painting

Leonardo is thought to have worked on *The Baptism of Christ*, a major painting produced by Verrocchio's workshop. Both tempera and oil paint were used in it. Tempera, the old way of painting pictures on wooden panels, involved mixing powdered pigment with egg yolk, wine vinegar, and water. The paint was applied in a series of quick-drying layers to build up the desired shades. Oil paint was new to Italy, having been developed in northern Europe in the early fifteenth century. It was easier to apply and allowed the artist to create more subtle shading. Leonardo was one of the first artists to use oil painting in Italy.

▶ The guilds were generous supporters of the arts. The wool refiners of Florence sponsored the competition for the design of the famous bronze doors of the Baptistery, which was won by this panel, The Sacrifice of Isaac (1401–02) by Lorenzo Ghiberti (1378–1455).

The Guild System

In 1472, Leonardo became a member of the Compagnia di San Luca, Florence's famous guild for artists. It was named after St. Luke, the patron saint of artists. All trades in medieval times had their own guilds. These powerful professional organizations maintained the standards of the trade, protected their members, and ensured that they got good prices for their products. Becoming a member of the Compagnia di San Luca shows that Leonardo, at age twenty, had completed his training and could become an independent professional artist.

Early Work

1469 Lorenzo de' Medici becomes ruler of Florence with his brother Giuliano.
c. 1474 Leonardo paints his portrait of *Ginevra de' Benci*.
c. 1476 Leonardo and three others are accused of illegal homosexual activities, for which the punishment might have been death. The case is dropped for lack of evidence.
1478 Giuliano de' Medici is assassinated. Lorenzo rules alone until his death in 1492. Leonardo receives his first commission as an independent artist, for an altarpiece for a chapel in the Palazzo della Signoria of Florence (the town hall of Florence), but he fails to complete the work.

Although, as a member of the Compagnia di San Luca, Leonardo was qualified to set up his own workshop, he continued to work in Verrocchio's workshop for at least another six years. The team-work involved in such workshops often meant that several artists worked on a painting. The paintings were not signed, so it is hard to know who contributed what. But it seems that Leonardo was put in charge of painting, and his influence and delicate artistic touch began to shine through.

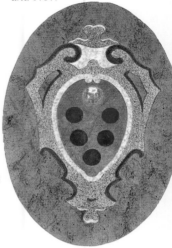

▼ *The Medici family coat of arms. Family members were merchants and bankers whose wealth brought them political power. They ruled Florence for most of the time between 1434 and 1737.*

Florence under the Medicis

Florence was the center of the art world and home to many of the best-known artists of the time. Many of them worked in Verrocchio's workshop. Florence was ruled by people who loved art, building, music, and scholarship. They felt that such things enhanced their prestige and were prepared to spend a lot of money on them. A key figure was the wealthy banker Lorenzo de' Medici (1449–92), the ruler of Florence also known as Lorenzo the Magnificent. The Medici family had dominated politics in the city since the 1430s.

◀ *Botticelli's* Adoration of the Magi *(c. 1475) includes portraits of the Medici.*

Florence in the Fifteenth Century

Florence had been a prosperous and powerful city since the twelfth century. During the fifteenth century, it developed into a major trading and manufacturing center and became one of the largest cities in Europe. Florence was one of a number of city-states in Italy. Others included Venice, Milan, Siena, Mantua, and Lucca. To show their wealth and power, the great city-states built magnificent churches, palaces, and public buildings. The best architects, painters, and sculptors of the day competed with each other to design and decorate these buildings.

Patrons of the Arts

During medieval times, the church was the biggest patron of the arts. As merchants and other citizens became richer, they also wanted to commission works of art. In Leonardo's time, patrons were changing from the church to rulers and private citizens. Religious scenes still remained the main subject for paintings.

▶ The Madonna of Mercy *(c. 1472) by Domenico Ghirlandaio. The Virgin Mary is shown protecting members of the wealthy Vespucci family of Florence.*

Religious Art

Christianity remained the central belief system in Europe during the Renaissance, despite the fact that scholars were studying the art, literature, and philosophy of the ancient Romans and Greeks, whose civilizations developed before Christianity. People were concerned with big questions, such as how to live one's life and what happens when we die. They found their answers in Christianity. The stories of the Bible and the lives of the saints seemed to contain lessons and examples that were relevant to their lives. It was the job of artists to turn these stories into visual images.

▶ Deposition (c. 1437–40), an altarpiece by Fra Angelico (c. 1400–55), shows the moment when Christ was taken down from the cross.

▲ Leonardo's pen-and-ink drawing of the Madonna and Child with a Cat (c. 1478) may have been done as a preparatory sketch for a painting now lost.

Altarpieces

The main focus of a church is the altar, and many of the most important works of art were designed to decorate altars. Altarpieces were commissioned by churches, monasteries, and other institutions. Altarpieces were also bought by wealthy individuals; they hoped that prayers said in front of their altarpieces would help their souls in the afterlife.

Leonardo's Madonnas

Most of Leonardo's early paintings are on religious subjects. He painted at least two versions of the Madonna and Child. It was a subject that he returned to throughout his career. At this time, he also began painting a facial expression — calm, thoughtful, mysterious — that is echoed in most of his later paintings.

▶ The Madonna with the Carnation is believed to have been painted by Leonardo while he was still working in Verrocchio's workshop in about 1474.

The Successful Artist

c. 1478 Leonardo leaves Verrocchio to set up his own workshop. He probably meets Ludovico Sforza, his future patron, in Milan. The first pages of his codices (books of notes) date from this time. Botticelli paints for the Medici family.
1480 Leonardo is reportedly working for Lorenzo de' Medici.
1481 He is commissioned to paint the *Adoration of the Magi* for the church of San Donato a Scopeto near Florence.
1482 Leonardo moves to Milan, leaving the *Adoration of the Magi* unfinished.

▶ *It is possible that Verrocchio's statue of David (c. 1475) was based on a portrait of Leonardo, who was then twenty-three.*

As commissions came flooding in from patrons, Leonardo set up his own workshop. At this early stage of his career, he was already beginning to encounter a problem that would recur throughout his life — his inability to complete a project. In his time, it was fashionable to show a multitude of talents in a wide variety of pursuits. Leonardo was not only a brilliant artist, he was also a good musician and horseman. He was charming and generous but also appears to have been a rather solitary figure. During his life, he seems to have developed his closest relationships with his students.

The Young Leonardo

Little is known for certain about Leonardo's personality or what he looked like. Records suggest that he cut a striking figure, with long flowing hair and blue eyes, and that he was proud of his good looks. It has been suggested that the figure on the far right of his *Adoration of the Magi* is a self-portrait. He loved animals and was apparently vegetarian. Interestingly, he was ambidextrous: he wrote with his left hand but could draw with both hands.

The Artist in Society

As the Renaissance progressed, the status of artists in society rose. Under the old guild and workshop system, artists were often seen as craftsmen and remained anonymous, but increasingly, leading independent artists were becoming famous as individuals, recognized for their own styles. Competition was fierce. Leonardo was competing for work with a large number of leading artists, including Botticelli and Verrocchio.

◀ *The Three Muses are depicted in* La Primavera, *or* The Spring *(1478–82), painted by Botticelli (1445–1510). His work represented a real break from tradition because he made large paintings about subjects from classical Greece and Rome, not from the Bible.*

▲ *A pottery plaque made in about 1465 by Lucca Della Robbia (c. 1400–82) at the guilds' church of Orsanmichele in Florence.*

Perspective

This preliminary study from the *Adoration of the Magi* shows how Leonardo planned the background. Lines drawn on the ground all lead to a single point on the horizon called the vanishing point. This was a technique devised by Brunelleschi in Florence to draw perspective. It was described in 1436 in a book by the architect, artist, and writer Leon Battista Alberti (1404-72). Without this technique, Leonardo would have found it very difficult to draw his double flights of steps convincingly.

The *Adoration of the Magi*

Leonardo's biggest commission at this time came from the monks of San Donato a Scopeto near Florence. The subject was the *Adoration of the Magi*. Leonardo was paid in advance and was to complete the picture in less than two and a half years. He made many preparatory drawings and drew the composition on the panel but never got any further. Despite this, we can see that it was an ambitious piece. Highly emotional figures in the background contrast with the calm figures in the center arranged in a triangular or pyramidal composition. These elements would recur in his later paintings.

▲ *Leonardo's* Adoration of the Magi *was begun in 1481 but never finished. All we see is the brown underpaint on a wooden panel almost 6.5 square feet (about 2 square meters).*

1476 Duke Galeazzo Maria Sforza, ruler of Milan, is assassinated and succeeded by his nine-year-old son Gian Galleazzo.

1480 Ludovico Sforza ousts Gian Galleazzo, his nephew, to become ruler of Milan.

c. 1482 Leonardo goes to Milan. Possibly also this year, he composes a letter (undated) to Ludovico Sforza, listing his accomplishments, in the hope of winning Sforza's patronage.

1483 He concludes a contract for the *Virgin of the Rocks*.

1484–6 Plague kills one third of the population of Milan; this inspires Leonardo to think about designing an ideal city.

1487 Leonardo receives payment for a wooden model for the lantern tower of Milan cathedral.

1488 Leonardo's friend Donato Bramante is in Pavia, working as consultant on the new cathedral. Verrocchio dies.

To Milan

Leonardo was apparently running a successful workshop in Florence when he left for Milan in about 1482. He spent much of the next eighteen years in Milan, working for Duke Ludovico Sforza (1452–1508). Known as Ludovico *il Moro*, he came from a family of mercenaries. The Sforzas had taken over power in Milan in 1450, and Ludovico had won his position through political schemes, making many enemies. He saw himself as a Renaissance prince and had ambitions to build Milan's reputation as a center of culture and power. Leonardo, it seems, saw new opportunities at Ludovico's court.

▲ *A gold coin of Galeazzo Maria Sforza, the elder brother of Ludovico, who was assassinated in 1476.*

Milan Under the Sforzas

Like many of the Renaissance rulers, Ludovico Sforza was an ambitious, ruthless, and tough politician and warrior. He was also extremely vain. He was eager to build around himself and his court all the fashionable cultural trappings of the Renaissance and to create an ideal city-state. He gathered together a number of leading artists, architects, and scholars.

The Move to Milan

Why Leonardo stayed on in Milan is not known for certain. As a courtier to Ludovico Sforza, he would receive a salary that would allow him the financial security to pursue his other ideas. To this end, he wrote a letter to Sforza listing his talents. Milan was at war with Venice at the time; the city was also a major manufacturer of weapons. In his letter, Leonardo stated that first and foremost, he was a military engineer, capable of building extraordinary new pieces of military equipment. At the end of his list, he mentioned that he could serve as an architect, painter, and sculptor. In due course, he was appointed official painter and engineer to the duke.

Renaissance Music

Leonardo may have been sent to Milan by Lorenzo de' Medici to act as a kind of cultural ambassador, and some reports suggest that he came bearing gifts that included a musical instrument, a precious lyre. Leonardo himself is believed to have been a good singer and player of the lyre. Music played a central role in Renaissance courts and was part of the international exchange of culture in Europe.

▲ *Leonardo's* Portrait of a Musician *(c. 1490). This was formerly thought to be a portrait of Ludovico Sforza.*

▶ *Renaissance musicians used a mixture of instruments, including the keyboard harpsichord, viols, cellos, and various wind instruments.*

The *Virgin of the Rocks*

One of the first major paintings undertaken by Leonardo in Milan was the *Virgin of the Rocks*, commissioned by the chapel of the Confraternity of the Immaculate Conception. He began work on it in 1483. It was the central panel of three; the other two panels, with angels, were completed by his workshop colleagues, the brothers Evangelista and Giovan Ambrogio de' Predis. Full of compassion, dignity, and tranquility, it was one of Leonardo's most successful paintings. Leonardo used his new sfumato technique, in which a very subtle passage from light to shadow almost eliminates the outlines of the drawing, creating very smooth figures and a sense of atmosphere in the space. As was a common practice in those days, Leonardo made another copy of this painting, which was completed by his collaborators in about 1508.

◄ *The* Virgin of the Rocks *(c. 1483–86) shows the Virgin, Jesus, John the Baptist, and an angel.*

▼ Scheme for Palaces and Roads at Various Levels *(c. 1488) shows his plans for an innovative multilevel town. It may have been a design for Milan.*

Leonardo the Architect

Leonardo's many duties in Milan included designing buildings and giving his advice to other architects. He was fortunate to have as a colleague in Milan the gifted architect and painter Donato Bramante (1444–1514), who brought a new look to Renaissance architecture, strongly influenced by the architecture of ancient Greece and Rome. When Bramante was commissioned to design the new cathedral for Pavia, Leonardo lent a hand. However, although Leonardo made numerous drawings of churches, palaces, and fortresses, no complete building exists today that was definitely designed by him.

▲ *A modern model of a centrally planned church, based on Leonardo's drawings dating from about 1488.*

▼ *The* Ideal City *(1480), by an unknown artist, shows a precise perspective and symmetrical composition.*

The Ideal City

Italian cities had medieval origins and were full of narrow, crowded, and dark streets. Like many architects of his day, Leonardo was fascinated by the concept of an Ideal City — a spacious, hygienic city of perfect design. Designs for such cities tended to be based on ancient Roman and Greek styles. Leonardo took the idea one step further by planning a city on a series of levels, each with its own function and means of transportation.

The Portrait Painter

1489 Leonardo designs the sets for the festivities celebrating the wedding of Ludovico Sforza's nephew Gian Galeazzo Sforza and Isabella of Aragon.
1490 Salaí joins Leonardo's household. Leonardo paints his portrait of Cecilia Gallerani *(The Lady with the Ermine)* at about this time.
1491 Ludovico Sforza marries Beatrice d'Este. Leonardo designs the costumes for the parade and sets for the festivities.
1494 Ludovico Sforza is officially granted the title of Duke of Milan. Leonardo carries out land reclamation work in Vigévano, birthplace of Ludovico Sforza, and perhaps designs the ducal palace.

One of Leonardo's duties as a court painter was to paint the portraits of the nobles and their families. Leonardo was a gifted portraitist. He practiced his drawing constantly, studying all kinds of facial types, expressions, and emotions; his drawings include some of his most remarkable work. In his paintings, he applied his subtle shading technique (sfumato) to the faces and made scientific studies on the effect of light on skin. In addition, he delved into what lay beneath the surface, studying the structure of the human body by dissecting dead bodies.

Sketches and Observation

Leonardo was fascinated by the nature of beauty. He drew a large number of pictures of grotesque faces. He also made detailed studies of beauty, especially the kind of feminine beauty that we see in his Madonnas. He was intrigued by the idea that an artist might be able to portray not just what people look like, but also their personalities. Leonardo's drawings were done on paper, in ink or chalk, or with a technique called metalpoint or silverpoint using a fine instrument like a pencil.

Leonardo's Academy

In Milan, Leonardo may have been in charge of a large workshop called Achademia Leonardi Vinci. His colleagues and pupils included Giovanni Antonio Boltraffio (c. 1467–1516), Ambrogio de Predis (c. 1455–c. 1508), Francesco Galli (called "Napoletano," died in the early sixteenth century), Andrea Solari (active 1495–1524), and Marco d'Oggiono (c. 1475–1530). In 1490, they were joined by a young boy called Gian Giacomo Caprotti da Oreno. Leonardo treated him like a son, but he was such a rascal that he earned the nickname Salaí, meaning devil. Salaí was one of his most loyal supporters, and he stayed with Leonardo almost to the end of his life.

▲ *Leonardo explored a variety of facial expressions in his* Five Grotesque Heads *(1485–90) It shows a man dressed like a Roman emperor being mocked by those around him.*

▶ *The emblem of the* Achademia Leonardi Vinci *(1495) shows a face in profile, similar in many respects to the drawing of the "emperor" above.*

Portraiture

During the fifteenth century, it was fashionable for Italian nobles to have their portraits painted in profile. Although Leonardo did drawings of profiles, he used the three-quarter view for his paintings. This was a northern European tradition used by Flemish painters. The angle especially suited his style and allowed him to explore shading and skin tones with greater subtlety. One of his most successful portraits — although much altered by later restorers — is believed to show Cecilia Gallerani, a mistress of Ludovico Sforza. It is also known as the *Lady with an Ermine*. The ermine (or stoat) that she holds creates an added mystery, but it seems to be explained by the fact that the Greek word for ermine (gale) resembled the sitter's name. There is also a strange correspondence between Cecilia's face and that of the ermine. Leonardo was fascinated with the idea that animals also showed emotion in their facial expressions. The painting is good evidence that Leonardo was equally talented at painting both humans and animals.

▶ *This portrait of a lady was painted by Fra Filippo Lippi (c. 1406–69) of Florence in about 1440, when it was fashionable to show the sitter from the side in profile.*

Symbols and Allegory

Paintings during Leonardo's time were full of symbols, which most viewers would have readily understood. For example, the lily held by the Angel Gabriel in the *Annunciation* (see page 8) is a symbol of purity, a reference to the Virgin Mary. Painters also liked to illustrate scenes from stories that were allegories, or symbols, with wider spiritual or moral meanings.

◀ The Ermine as a Symbol of Purity *(c. 1494), a pen and ink drawing by Leonardo. For Leonardo, the ermine represented purity: he believed that it would rather be taken by a hunter than escape into a dirty lair.*

Scientific Studies

Leonardo was a ceaseless investigator. Initially, his studies related to what he felt he needed to know for his work. He took a scientific approach, for example, to studying the gradations of light in shadow. In about 1487, he began taking part in the dissection of human bodies. This was unusual for doctors and was not strictly legal, but the church, and the law generally, turned a blind eye. It was very unusual, however, for an artist.

▶ *Leonardo's portrait of Cecilia Gallerani,* The Lady with the Ermine *(c. 1490).*

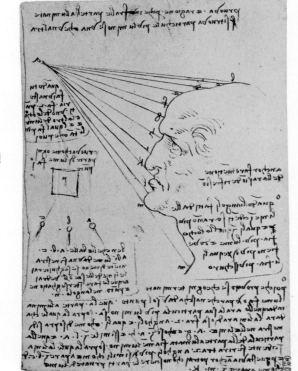

▶ Study of the Varying Effects of Light Striking a Profile from a Single Source *(1487–90).*

The Portrait Painter

▶ Leonardo's
Portrait of a
Musician (1490).

◄*One of Leonardo's best-known portraits of a woman, also known as* La Belle Ferronnière *(c. 1490).*

Painting and Science

1475 Early drawings by Leonardo show an interest in mechanics.
1487-93 Leonardo undertakes his first detailed anatomical studies, dissecting mainly animals.
c. 1490 He draws his *Vitruvian Man*.
c. 1493 He appears to have begun the second version of the *Virgin of the Rocks*.
1496 He begins mathematics studies with Luca Pacioli and assists him with his work on "divine proportion."
c. 1497 He begins his attempt to put his knowledge into a systematic order. This marks a shift from artist to scientist.

Leonardo was not a scholar; he was not given the kind of formal education he might have received if his parents had been married. He appears to have resented this, and he expressed a strong dislike of knowledge that came from books alone. To some extent, his lack of knowledge from books gave him a freedom to think for himself. He believed profoundly that the truth about the world could only be learned through careful observation and that all theories had to be tested against what could be seen and experienced in the real world. Always searching for answers in what he could see with his own eyes, he brought a fresh approach to whatever he studied.

▲ *A medieval illustration of the seven liberal arts with theology and philosophy placed at the center.*

▼ Plato *(c. 1480) as portrayed by the Spanish painter Pedro Berruguete (c. 1450–1504) in a series of paintings of Famous Men for the castle of Urbino, Italy.*

Intellectual Heritage

In Europe, up to and during the Renaissance, the most revered sources of information were the classical authors and scientists of ancient Greece and Rome. This meant that knowledge had barely progressed for a thousand years or so. The church dominated education, so all learning was closely connected to the teachings of the Bible. Learning at a higher level was divided into seven liberal arts (grammar, arithmetic, logic, music, astronomy, geometry, and rhetoric) plus the disciplines of theology and philosophy. During Leonardo's age, this old system was beginning to change as scholars began to look outside the teachings of the church. They also began to study texts by the old Greek and Roman writers, such as Plato and Aristotle, that revealed new and refreshing attitudes toward many subjects.

▶ *Early printing presses were based on the wine presses used to squeeze grapes. They pressed down on sheets of paper laid on top of inked lettering.*

The Printing Revolution

Up until 1455, European books were very rare and very expensive. Then in 1455, the German Johannes Gutenberg (c. 1395–1468) printed his first book. His real breakthrough was his use of moveable type: letters could be cast in metal, then arranged in sentences. From these letters, thousands of copies of a book could be printed easily. Suddenly, books became more plentiful and cheaper. This development had a huge impact on the spread of knowledge.

Humanism

For centuries, the church had taught that human beings were essentially sinful and would be condemned by God to eternal damnation after death unless they had led a virtuous life. The Renaissance changed this view. A way of thinking called humanism, based on the philosophy of the ancient Greeks and Romans, returned human beings to a state of dignity. They should be allowed to take control of their lives and their destiny and decide for themselves what was good or bad. The humanists encouraged individuality, free thinking, and open-mindedness.

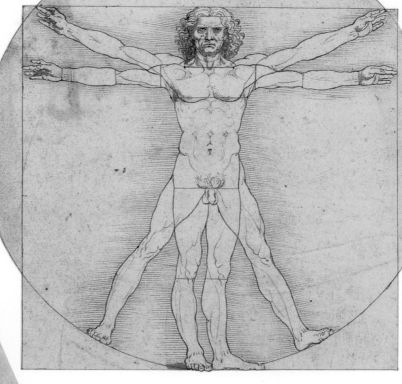

Leonardo's famous drawing, the Vitruvian Man *(c. 1490), is based on the work of the ancient Roman architect Vitruvius. It aims to demonstrate how perfect proportions in architecture relate to the human body. Note that the navel is at the center of the circle, and the crotch is at the center of the square.*

A page from one of Leonardo's notebooks showing his mirror writing. It is easy enough to decipher. The first word, for example, is Quanto *("how many").*

Leonardo's Notebooks

Throughout his career, Leonardo ceaselessly filled pages of paper with notes, drawings, comments, and scribbled sketches. He left some thirteen thousand pages of notes, only seven thousand of which have survived. These were later gathered together to form books called codices. With his left hand, Leonardo wrote from right to left, using mirror writing. This was not some kind of secret code; he just found it more convenient. His four main areas of study resulted in what are known as his Treatises, on painting, architecture, mechanics, and human anatomy. At one point, he developed the extraordinary ambition to capture all observed knowledge, hoping that this would yield the secrets of life itself. Of course, this was an impossible task.

Mathematics

During his stay in Milan, Leonardo made significant advances in learning mathematics, largely through the help of his friend, the mathematician Luca Pacioli (c. 1445–c. 1517). A Franciscan friar, Pacioli traveled around Italy lecturing in math and published some of the first European math books. Leonardo produced illustrations for Pacioli's book *On Divine Proportion* (1509). Although he showed no exceptional talent for the subject, Leonardo realized how mathematics underpins everything in the physical world. Mathematics helped him apply science to painting as well as to his designs in architecture and mechanics. Furthermore, he was convinced that divine harmony — in music, painting, and the world — has a mathematical basis.

Portrait of Fra Luca Pacioli (1495), probably by the Venetian artist Jacopo De' Barbari (c. 1440–1516). It shows the mathematician with one of his pupils.

Painting and Science

▲ *Perspective Study for the* Adoration of the Magi *(1481, see pages 12–13), in pen and ink on paper, shows the perspective grid that helped Leonardo judge the correct angles and scale in the painting.*

War and Warriors

One project that Leonardo discussed from the very beginning of his stay in Milan was Ludovico Sforza's idea of building a statue to his father, Francesco Sforza (1401–66). From the outset, the plan was to build a huge equestrian monument. Since Roman times, such statues were considered highly desirable statements about power and domination. Initially, Leonardo planned to create a statue of a horse rearing up on its hind legs, but it proved impossible to produce on a large scale. Faced with these difficulties, Leonardo kept putting the project off.

▼ This fresco painting by Andrea del Castagno (1421–57), Pippo Spano (c. 1450), shows a mercenary dressed in armor designed for mounted warfare.

The Warring States

In Italy, the Renaissance was a turbulent time. The city-states were constantly at war. As ruling dynasties struggled for power, they raised armies, employed mercenaries, and built great fortresses and weapons. Successful war meant added power, prestige, and wealth. Leonardo was by nature a pacifist. He condemned war, but he clearly also accepted it as a necessary evil and devoted considerable energies to inventing weapons of terrifying destructive power.

Weapons

Leonardo had promised Sforza all kinds of new war machines, and his notebooks reveal his constant interest in pushing the boundaries of warfare. He drew plans for multibarrelled machine guns, giant bows, chariots armed with wheel-mounted scythes, and a kind of armored car or tank. Most of these designs proved impracticable during his time and were never built.

▲ A modern model based on Leonardo's sketch, drawn in about 1487, for a tanklike vehicle armed with twenty cannons. It was to be driven by men inside turning handles.

▼ An illustration from a manual on horsemanship shows three men breaking in a horse as the first stage of training it for warfare.

▶ A modern drawing based on Leonardo's sketch of a giant crossbow.

War Horses

Horses played a central role in the armies of the day and would continue to do so for another four centuries. War horses were carefully bred, trained for the task, and treasured as possessions of high prestige. Being good at riding was a considered a great virtue among warriors and humanists alike. Leonardo was said to be a good rider and was clearly fascinated by horses. He spent hours at the Sforza stables studying and sketching the physique of the horse.

▼ *Verrocchio's statue of Bartolomeo Colleoni (1400–75), a mercenary in the service of Venice. Based on ancient Roman models, this was the more typical pose for equestrian statues of the time.*

Bronze Casting

Leonardo's clay model would have been used to make the mold into which the molten bronze would have been poured. Casting such a huge statue in bronze presented real technical problems. Leonardo spent hours drawing up careful plans to show how it could be achieved.

▼ *A small bronze statue of a galloping horseman, attributed to Leonardo or his student Giovanni Francesco Rustici (1474–1554).*

The Equestrian Statue

The proposed statue of Francesco Sforza was a cherished project for Ludovico, who needed such a public statue as a symbol of his right to rule — he had, after all, taken power illegally. Leonardo was constantly reminded of the project but made little progress until about 1489. His main difficulty lay in mounting a huge bronze statue on two hind legs without additional support. In the end, he gave up his first idea and opted instead to build a more conventional statue but still on a huge scale. He started with the horse; we can presume that he intended to add the figure of the rider in a second stage. By 1493, he had produced a full-scale clay model of the horse that was over 23 feet (7 meters) tall.

▲ *A sketch by Leonardo of a rearing horse, possibly made as a study for the Sforza monument in about 1490.*

The Fate of the Sforza Monument

A total of 158,000 pounds (about 80 tons) of bronze was needed to cast Leonardo's horse. While preparations were being made for this major task, the clay horse was displayed in 1493 at the marriage of Ludovico's niece to Emperor Maximilian of Austria. It was praised as a breathtaking masterpiece. In 1494, the project ran into trouble. The French marched into Italy, causing chaos among the city-states. Anxious to strengthen their defenses, Ludovico Sforza sent the bronze that had been earmarked for the horse to Ferrara to make cannons. Thereafter, Ludovico was constantly short of funds, so the horse was never cast. The clay model was apparently destroyed in 1499 by French troops, who used it for target practice.

The Last Supper

1490 Ludovico Sforza makes alterations to the church of Santa Maria delle Grazie, which he adopts as his family burial place.
1495 Leonardo begins on the *Last Supper*.
1497 Ludovico Sforza's wife, Beatrice d'Este, dies suddenly. Sforza urges Leonardo to complete the *Last Supper*, but he refuses to be hurried.
1498 Completion of the *Last Supper*. Leonardo also completes ceiling decorations at the Sala delle Asse in the Castello Sforzesco in Milan (now much altered).

In 1495, Leonardo was invited to create a large mural for the refectory, or dining hall, of a monastery of Dominican friars in Milan, the Santa Maria delle Grazie. He took for his subject the Last Supper, a critical moment in the story of Christ and Christianity. Painted on a huge scale, this ambitious project was one of the most famous paintings of its day.

▼ *The church of Santa Maria delle Grazie in Milan as it appears today.*

▶ *Ludovico Sforza and his son, portrayed in the* Sforzesca Altarpiece *by an unknown painter in the late fifteenth century.*

▼ *A cartoon for a fresco. The outlines could be transferred to wet plaster by pricking them with a pin and rubbing powdered pigment through the holes.*

Santa Maria delle Grazie in Milan

This church and monastery, built between 1465 and 1482, had been adopted by the Sforzas as a place of worship and burial. Leonardo's task was to paint the end wall of the refectory. His plan was to make his painting look as though it formed part of the same room in which the monks were eating.

Fresco Painting

Traditionally, wall paintings in Italy were done using a method called *fresco*. Following a detailed plan, or cartoon, small areas of the painting were covered with damp plaster at the beginning of the day. Then water-based colors were painted onto it before the plaster dried. This produced a solid, durable finish, but it was a slow and inflexible way of working, and the colors were light and limited. This did not suit Leonardo, who wanted a method that could allow him to make changes as he went along and deepen tones for shading. He decided instead to use a mixture of oil paint and tempera on dry plaster — a new, untried technique.

The Composition

The paint techniques were not Leonardo's only innovation in the *Last Supper*. He also broke with tradition by placing the traitor, Judas, among the Disciples (leaning back, fourth from left). The scene is the moment when Christ unexpectedly announces that one of the Disciples present would betray him. The Disciples react with a variety of emotions, but the face of Christ — framed by the window and at the vanishing point of the architecture — creates a contrasting image of calm. The light on the Disciples' faces comes from Christ.

◄ *In this* Last Supper *(1480) by Ghirlandaio, Judas is placed in the traditional position, seated alone on the opposite side of the table from the other Disciples.*

▼ *In sketches of the Disciples, Leonardo explored various ways that their individual emotional reactions could be portrayed.*

Flawed Masterpiece

Leonardo's refusal to be hurried over the *Last Supper* angered his patrons. It is said that in a dispute with the abbot over his progress, Leonardo threatened to portray him as Judas. The painting was finally finished in 1498. Unfortunately, Leonardo's experimental paint technique and the infiltration of humidity in the wall did not allow it to keep its original beauty. The paint began to peel off as early as 1517, and by 1566, the whole painting was in a bad state.

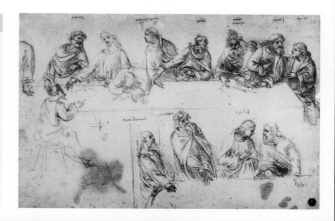

▼ *After centuries of deterioration, repainting, and restoration, the* Last Supper *(1495–98) became a ghost of the original, but its power and originality can still be clearly seen.*

To Mantua and Venice

1499 In July, the French army advances on Milan, and Ludovico Sforza flees to Austria. Milan falls to the French. In December, Leonardo travels to Mantua. He draws preparatory sketches for a portrait of Isabella d'Este (sister of Ludovico Sforza's wife). Outbreak of war between Venice and the Ottoman Empire (to 1503).
1500 In January, Ludovico Sforza's attempt to retake Milan fails; he is captured by the French. In March, Leonardo continues to Venice, where he stays for about six weeks.
1500 In April, Leonardo returns to Florence to much acclaim as a celebrated artist.

In 1499, Milan fell to the French, and Ludovico Sforza fled the city. Essentially the new king of France, Louis XII (1462–1515) had a claim to the Duchy of Milan through the Visconti, whom the Sforzas had pushed aside. For Leonardo, this was a personal disaster — he had lost his great patron. His reputation, however, was good. He set off on a search for a new patron — someone who would allow him to pursue his very broad range of interests. In this quest, he felt in no way constrained by past loyalties. Throughout his career, Leonardo appeared to show little unease about seeking clients among people who had been enemies of his former patrons.

Mantua

In December 1499, Leonardo left Milan, accompanied by Pacioli and a group of students. His first stop was Mantua, a city ruled by Duke Francesco II (1466–1519) of the Gonzaga family. Mantua was a famous center for the arts. The court artist, Andrea Mantegna (c. 1430–1506), painted the celebrated frescoes in the Castello di San Giorgio.

▲ *The sons of Frederico Gonzaga are portrayed in this detail of a painting by Mantegna.*

Women as Patrons

Isabella d'Este (1474–1539) was one of a number of women who played a significant role in the arts during the Italian Renaissance. From her position of power as the wife of Duke Francesco II, she was able to exert influence on the court. Isabella, one of the most brilliant and scholarly women of the time, was also a forceful patron. After Leonardo produced his first pastel portrait of her, she badgered him relentlessly for an oil version of it and offered him other commissions but in vain.

▲ *Isabella d'Este's medallion. She gave copies of this to poets whom she admired.*

▲ *Leonardo's* Portrait of Isabella d'Este *(c. 1500), drawn in charcoal and pastel. The outlines have been pricked to transfer the image to a finished painting, but if the painting was ever completed, it was lost.*

Venice

In March 1500, Leonardo and Pacioli went on to Venice — a long-time enemy of Milan. At this time, Venice was at the height of its powers. A great trading city, it had colonies and contacts across the eastern half of the Mediterranean. It was also an unusual city, built on a series of marshy islands in the middle of a lagoon and threaded by a network of canals that served as roads. Much of the wealth of the traders was invested in fine buildings and in the arts. During the sixteenth century, it became even more important than Florence as an artistic center. Some of the greatest painters in Italy at the time of Leonardo were based there, including Giovanni Bellini (c. 1430–1516) and Giorgione (c. 1477–1510), who was much impressed by Leonardo's work.

◀ Portrait of Doge Leonardo Loredan (c. 1501) by Giovanni Bellini. Despite the impression given by his outfit, the Doge, ruler of Venice, was not a Church figure but an elected citizen.

◀ A fifteenth-century view of St. Mark's Square in Venice showing the Campanile (bell tower) in the center, St. Mark's Cathedral at the top left, and next to it, the Doges' Palace.

◀ The janissaries were the elite troops of the Ottoman army.

The Ottoman Empire

Venice was under threat from another great power of the eastern Mediterranean, the Ottoman Empire. Based in present-day Turkey, the Muslim sultans of the Ottoman Empire had captured many of the old Christian lands and cities of the eastern Mediterranean, including, in 1453, Constantinople (now Istanbul), the capital of the Byzantine Empire. Now the Ottoman Empire threatened Venice itself in a war that lasted from 1499 to 1503. When Leonardo reached Venice, Turkish warships lay off the coast, and the Turkish army was encamped just outside the city. Leonardo, therefore, offered his services as a military engineer.

Underwater Defenses

Leonardo's suggestions were highly inventive. He proposed to flood the Turks by means of an ingenious mobile wooden dam slung across a valley. He also produced designs for a kind of submarine, a deep-sea diving suit, and shoe attachments to walk on water. His proposed underwater breathing apparatus was designed to permit soldiers to walk on the seabed. He pictured a kind of aquatic army equipped so that soldiers could advance on the enemy fleet and drill holes in their ships. As with so many of his inventions, however, these ideas were not really practicable and were never realized.

▼ One of Leonardo's designs for diving equipment involved breathing tubes leading up to an air inlet that floated on the surface.

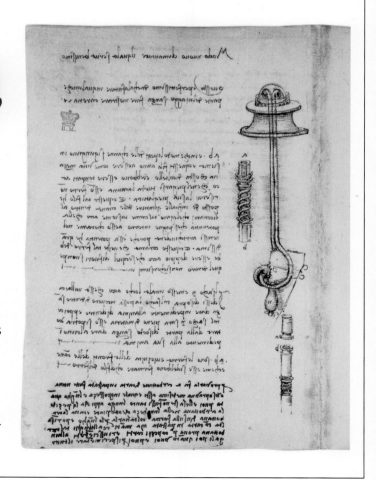

Military Architect and Mapmaker

1501 In Florence, Leonardo completes his *Madonna with the Yarnwinder* (known only through copies) for the king of France, Louis XII. Leonardo is reportedly too distracted by his mathematical experiments to paint.
1502 He works for Cesare Borgia for nine months as senior military architect and general engineer.
1503 Cesare Borgia falls from power on the death of his father. Leonardo devises projects to divert the course of the Arno River during the siege of Pisa. Work begins in **1504** but is soon abandoned.

Leonardo returned to Florence in April 1500 and lived at the Monastery of Santissima Annunziata. There he was commissioned to paint the *Virgin and Child with St. Anne*, a project he failed to complete. In 1502, Leonardo began work as architect and engineer for Cesare Borgia (1475–1507), a brutal, cunning military ruler who was widely detested. It seemed like an odd choice, but Leonardo still desperately needed a patron.

◀ Portrait of Cesare Borgia by Altobello Meloni *(c. 1490–1543). Cesare was said to be the model for Machiavelli's* The Prince.

▶ *A nineteenth-century statue of Machiavelli by Lorenzo Bartolini.*

Cesare Borgia
Cesare Borgia was the illegitimate son of Pope Alexander VI (1431–1503), who was widely criticized as being corrupt. Cesare was given the Duchy of Romagna and was the Commander-in-Chief of the Papal army. It is possible that Leonardo resigned after a cruel incident in which his friend Vitellozzo Vitelli, an army officer, was treacherously murdered under Borgia's orders.

Machiavelli
During this period, Leonardo met Niccolò Machiavelli (1469–1527), secretary and second chancellor to the Florentine Republic. He was a writer of plays, history, and political theory. His most famous book, *The Prince* (1513), offers advice to rulers about how to gain and keep power through ruthless cunning. It is said to be based on Cesare Borgia.

Fortifications
Working for Borgia, Leonardo traveled around Romagna, Emilia, the Marches, Umbria, and Tuscany, studying the cities and fortresses and supervising building work. Warfare was changing rapidly with the increasing power of cannons. Fortresses now had to be redesigned. Instead of high walls, low, angled stone-fronted walls were set out in a star shape. Leonardo's drawings of fortresses show him grappling with this problem.

◀*Leonardo's sketch for a fortress, dating from about 1502, shows the kind of earthworks, low walls, and star shape adopted to resist cannon fire.*

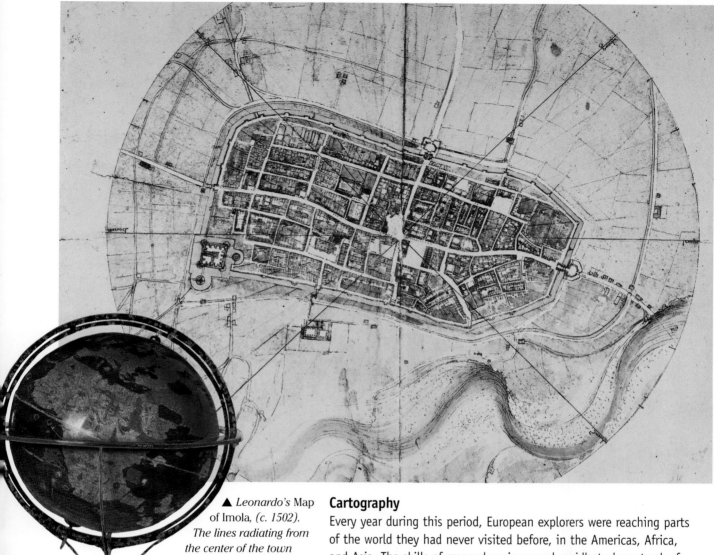

▲ *Leonardo's* Map
of Imola, *(c. 1502).*
The lines radiating from
the center of the town
mark the eight points
of the compass.

◀ *This globe, made in about*
1502, shows an attempt to map
the new discoveries around Africa
and in the Indian Ocean.

Cartography

Every year during this period, European explorers were reaching parts of the world they had never visited before, in the Americas, Africa, and Asia. The skills of mapmakers improved rapidly to keep track of these discoveries. Leonardo made maps using an aerial view based on directions fixed with a magnetic compass and measurements paced out on the ground. His map of Imola was the most accurate town plan of its day, far more accurate than the usual sketch plan. With his combination of art and science, he set a new standard for cartography.

Water Projects

Leonardo had long been convinced that the Arno River could be adapted to link Florence to the sea, a major project that required skills in mapping, studies in water flow, and engineering. The plan was of military interest to Florence, which was at war with Pisa, because diverting the river could deprive Pisa of access to the sea. In 1503, Leonardo drew a number of maps for the project, but it soon was abandoned.

▶ *Leonardo's sketch for an earthmoving*
machine (c. 1480) designed for digging out
trenches for canals. His ambitious plans for
diverting the Arno River were never realized.

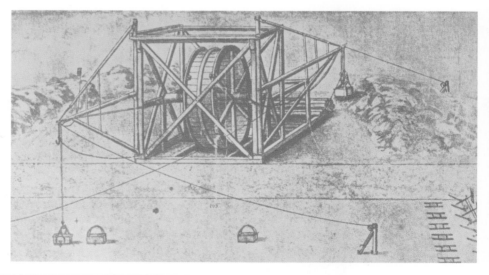

Mystery and Myth

Back in Florence in 1503, Leonardo returned to painting and produced his most famous portrait, the *Mona Lisa*. It shows many of his characteristic techniques: the use of light and deep shadow and smoky shading (sfumato), which softens the outlines of the face. Few paintings of the time match this portrait for its wonder. Leonardo was attempting to capture "the emotions of her mind and the passions of her soul." This was apparently Leonardo's favorite painting.

c. 1500 Leonardo works on a cartoon of the *Virgin, Child, St. Anne and St. John the Baptist*.
1503 Back in Florence, Leonardo rejoins the Compagnia di San Luca. He begins painting the *Mona Lisa*.
1504 He makes the first studies for his lost painting *Leda and the Swan*. Isabella d'Este apparently commissions Leonardo to paint a *Young Christ*.
Ser Piero, Leonardo's father, dies at age 80.
1506 He reportedly finishes the *Mona Lisa* but keeps it.

The Mystery of the Mona Lisa

Leonardo himself was fond of this painting, and it remained in his possession until the end of his life. This in itself is a mystery because usually a portrait would be handed over to the person who commissioned it. Who is the sitter? Nobody knows for sure. Another name for the painting is *La Gioconda*, which means "the merry woman," but it could be the wife of a silk merchant called Francesco del Giacondo. Many other suggestions have been put forward, some plausible, some far-fetched — including that this is really a self-portrait of Leonardo.

Leonardo's Paintings of Women

The triumph of the *Mona Lisa* is that she looks real, with emotions that convey themselves directly to the viewer. She has a calm, self-assured presence. She shares much with the other women in Leonardo's paintings, notably the Madonnas. Leonardo was clearly attracted to this concept of the ideal woman.

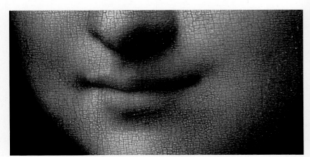

▲ *The famous smile is delicately shaded and slightly lopsided, creating an impression of flickering, living emotion.*

▶ *The* Mona Lisa *is now probably the world's most famous painting.*

A detail from Hercules and the Hydra (c. 1470) shows the Florentine painter Antonio Pollaiuolo (c. 1432–1498) exploring a theme from classical mythology.

▲ Arno Landscape (1473). Leonardo sketched landscapes from early in his career and is credited with some of the first pure landscape pictures.

Fantasy Landscape

The background of the *Mona Lisa* also lends an air of mystery. Leonardo liked to paint these dreamy landscapes, seen especially in the *Virgin of the Rocks*. They create the impression of timelessness and the power of nature. The background to the *Mona Lisa* bears a strong resemblance to the rocky landscape in the valleys of the Chiana and Arno Rivers, which Leonardo visited when working for Cesare Borgia. The bridge seen just above the sitter's left shoulder is thought to be based on the Buriano bridge near Arezzo. Leonardo was fascinated by geology and concluded that the creative forces behind rock formation must be more complex than the explanations given in *The Bible*.

Mythology

In about 1504, Leonardo began work on a painting called *Leda and the Swan*. He made a number of sketches, but his painting has been lost and is known only through copies. The subject concerns the old Greek myth of a Queen of Sparta who was seduced by the god Zeus in the form of a swan. Many of Leonardo's sketches explore this kind of story, in which myth and the real world combine. The stories of ancient Rome and Greece provided a rich source for such subject matter.

Study of Two Plants for the Leda (c. 1508–10) by Leonardo. Similar plants appear at the foot of the Florence Leda.

◄ A detail of Leda and the Swan *from the copy in Florence (1508–15). Leda has a typical Leonardo face.*

Nature Studies

Part of the attraction of mythological subjects for Leonardo must have been the way he could combine imagination with his observations of nature. Throughout his life, he sketched plants, animals, and landscapes. He had a relentlessly inquiring mind, and he wanted to find out the secrets that lay behind everything in the world. He also studied anatomy by dissecting corpses at the hospital of Santa Maria Nuova in Florence.

The Art of War

▼ *The central figure of the left panel of Uccello's* Battle of San Romano *(c. 1455) is the general Niccolò da Tolentino leading the Florentine troops to victory over Siena.*

Leonardo also undertook a second vast mural project at this time, for the council chamber of the Palazzo Vecchio of Florence. The subject was the Battle of Anghiari, a famous historic victory of the Florentines over Milan in 1440. The mural, if completed, would have been one of the most magnificent painting projects ever because the great Michelangelo (1475–1564) was working on a companion piece, the *Battle of Cascina*, showing the victory of Florence over Pisa.

▶ *The Palazzo Vecchio, Florence, as it appears today.*

The Art of War

The great cultural achievements of the Renaissance all took place against a backdrop of constant warfare and violence. Paintings depicting war tended to glorify or to celebrate the bravery and victory of the combatants. The *Battle of San Romano*, painted by the Florentine painter Paolo Uccello (1397–1475) for the Medici Palace, shows stylized figures in an idealized scene.

The Palazzo Vecchio

This palace, in the center of Florence, was the headquarters of the city government. Originally a medieval building dating from 1298–1314, it had been updated and restored over the years. The Salone dei Cinquecento (Hall of the Five Hundred) was added in the 1490s as a new council chamber. There could hardly have been a more important, higher-profile location for a major painting.

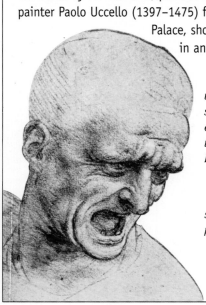

◀ *The drawing of a warrior by Leonardo shows the intense emotion he planned to convey in the* Battle of Anghiari.

▶ *A sketch gives some idea of the planned composition.*

Rivalry

While Leonardo was thoughtful, organized, elegant, cultivated, and tidy, Michelangelo was passionate, rude, boastful, and dirty. Michelangelo hated and despised Leonardo and mocked him for never finishing anything. Michelangelo had completed his magnificent *Pietà*, the great masterpiece of his younger years, for St. Peter's in Rome in about 1499. He was considered by many to be the greatest artist of the day. He started work on the *Battle of Cascina* in 1504, but when he left for Rome the following year, he had finished only the cartoons.

▲ Michelangelo's Battle of Cascina *is known only through versions by other artists based on the cartoon. This version, attributed to Sebastiano da Sangallo (1481-1551), dates from 1542.*

The Battle of Anghiari

We do not know exactly what Leonardo intended for his *Battle of Anghiari*. Once again, he attempted to use an experimental kind of paint — this time oil paint on plaster — but it was so unstable that it failed even to dry. A fire lit to dry the paint apparently just caused it to run. Our knowledge of it comes from his sketches and from copies made of the cartoon. It is clear from these that Leonardo intended to create an image of immense energy and emotion.

The David Controversy

As Michelangelo completed his statue of *David*, a committee assembled to decide where best to put it. Among them was Leonardo. The majority thought it should go under a loggia, but Michelangelo wanted a more prominent position. Michelangelo seems to have held a grudge against Leonardo for voting against his wish.

▶ Michelangelo's David *(1504), one of the most famous pieces of Renaissance sculpture, was carved from a single block of marble.*

▲ The Battle of Anghiari *(c. 1603) by Peter Paul Rubens (1577–1640). Several versions were made by artists based on Leonardo's lost cartoon.*

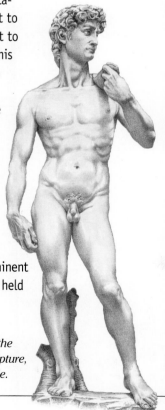

Back in Milan

In 1506, Leonardo was invited back to Milan by Charles d'Amboise, the French governor. Leonardo spent most of the next six years there. In 1507, he became court painter to Louis XII of France (1462–1515), who was then residing in Milan. It was perhaps an odd move, for he was effectively siding with the enemies of his former patron Ludovico Sforza, but it seems that Leonardo considered himself a free agent. He returned to Florence from time to time. In the winter of 1507–08, for instance, he visited Florence to help his friend Giovanni Francesco Rustici.

▲ *The sculpture by Giovanni Francesco Rustici, the* Preaching of St. John the Baptist *(1506–11), sit above the north door of the Baptistery in Florence It is said to be based on drawings by Leonardo.*

▶ Masquerader *(c. 1512). Leonardo's notebooks contain a number of costume designs for court entertainment.*

Costumes

Entertainment in Renaissance courts was spectacular, involving numerous participants in inventive costumes. There were acrobats, jugglers, musicians, and dancers. To make the entertainment even more spectacular, fantastic mechanical devices were created, such as whales that could open their mouths to devour actors. Leonardo was particularly fond of gimmicks, practical jokes, and fanciful theatrical machinery. He even tried to create a mechanical human being as a court entertainment.

Court Painter

Leonardo had found a devoted patron and revered status working for Louis XII. In this period in Milan, he worked mainly on notebooks and studied anatomy. To have help with his duties as a court painter, he continue to run a workshop, which included de Predis and Salaí. Francesco Melzi (1493–1570) joined the workshop and became Leonardo's faithful companion to the end.

Gardens

Leonardo designed a villa for Charles d'Amboise that was never built. He put considerable effort into designing the garden. Fed by the city canals, it was to contain waterfalls, fountains, musical watermills, a water-operated clock, and spurts of water designed to shoot out unexpectedly at passersby. Inspired by descriptions of ancient Roman gardens, this sort of garden was fashionable at the time.

▶ *The gardens of the Villa Farnese, near Rome, were set out in the early sixteenth century. This fountain with figures of river gods is typical of the elaborate garden ornaments of the day.*

Virgin and Child with St. Anne

Leonardo produced very few paintings during this period. He and his workshop completed the second version of the *Virgin of the Rocks* in 1508. Two years later, he finished another great masterpiece, *Virgin and Child with St. Anne*. It shows the Virgin Mary sitting on the lap of her mother, St. Anne, while reaching for the child Jesus, who is playing with a lamb. The complex composition of the figures is set against a background of distant mountains, showing Leonardo's mastery of aerial perspective with the blue layering of landscape into the distance.

Study of Drapery for Virgin and Child with St. Anne *(c. 1508–10). Accurate drawing of cloth was one of Leonardo's great skills. He wanted clothing to look as though it covered a real body.*

▲ The Virgin and Child with St. Anne *is perhaps Leonardo's most powerful depiction of motherhood, one of his enduring themes.*

◀ Study for the Trivulzio Monument *(c. 1511) shows that Leonardo imagined a very grand and impressive monument.*

Tombs

Another of Leonardo's duties was to design public monuments. In about 1511, he worked on a grand equestrian tomb for Marshal Gian Giacomo Trivulzio (c. 1441–1518), the viceroy of Milan, who had planned to spend a large sum of money for the creation of his tomb and monument. Once again, Leonardo played with the idea of depicting a rearing horse, this time with the raised front legs supported by a fallen enemy. Leonardo drew a number of sketches, but the monument itself was never completed.

The Human Body and Mechanics

1507 Leonardo dissects the body of a man of one hundred whose death he had witnessed in the hospital of Santa Maria Nuova in Florence.
1509 A treatise on the Golden Section, *De Divina Proportione* by mathematician Luca Pacioli, is published with Leonardo's illustrations.
1510 Leonardo carries out dissections with Marcantonio della Torre at the University of Pavia.
1513 Massimiliano Sforza, son of Ludovico, takes back Milan with the help of the Swiss, the Papal Armies, and Venice. Leonardo leaves Milan to stay on the Melzi estate at Vaprio nearby. The Medici family returns to power in Florence under Lorenzo di Piero de' Medici, grandson of Lorenzo the Magnificent.

In Milan, Leonardo continued his studies of anatomy, now focusing more on the mechanics of the human body and his search for the location of the soul. He was assisted by a leading anatomist of Pavia, Marcantonio della Torre (1473–1511). It was only with the next generation, led by the Flemish anatomist Andreas Vesalius (1514–64) working in Padua, that anatomy began to be properly understood. Meanwhile, medical knowledge remained generally backward.

▶ *A late-sixteenth-century ivory figure based on the work of Vesalius, made to demonstrate how the organs of the body function.*

Anatomical Studies

When Leonardo first started to dissect corpses, it was in quest of greater knowledge of the human body so he could be able to paint the human form. By this time, his research went far beyond the needs of his painting. Leonardo always believed in the power of the artist to reveal the truth through observation and accurate drawing. Here his argument was proven. His anatomical drawings were better than any other in his day. He introduced various new ways of drawing diagrams and cross sections, laying the foundations of modern medical illustration. Also new was the way that he combined words and illustration so each complemented the other.

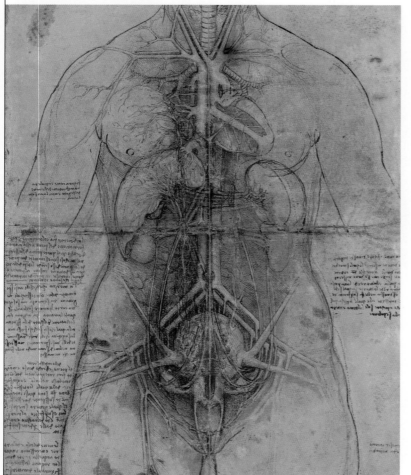

▶ Embryo in the Womb
(c. 1512). Leonardo was the first to draw detailed studies of the human embryo.

◀ *Leonardo's anatomical study of a woman's body, dating from about 1507. No one had drawn the female body in such detail before. It is interesting to compare this with the much later ivory figure above.*

Medicine

It took some courage to dissect corpses. Apart from the unpleasantness of the process, which for religious reasons had to be conducted at night, such activities were regarded with deep suspicion. But through this work, Leonardo acquired a far deeper knowledge of the human body. Medicine was still largely based on the works of classical doctors, such as Galen (c. 129–c. 199) — who never dissected a body — and later Arab scholars. Leonardo's research did little to improve medicine. For one thing, that was not his purpose; for another, his drawings and notes were not published until much later.

▲ The basis for medicine was the work of the ancient Greeks. This illustration shows how to bandage a head injury.

The Mechanics of the World

Leonardo had a profound belief that mechanics were the key to the structure of the universe and that the weather, the stars, and river systems could all be accounted for in terms of mechanics. The human body, he concluded, was the "ultimate machine," an advanced system working on the same principles as hinges, pulleys, winches, levers, hoists, canals, and water mills.

▼ A model based on one of Leonardo's sketches of a flying machine: a glider inspired by bat wings.

▼ Study for a Flying-Machine (1483–86). This sketch for a helicopterlike flying machine with spiral rotor was perhaps based on a child's paper toy, a whirligig on a stick. The weight of the four pilots, however, would have been far too great to lift the machine by muscle power alone.

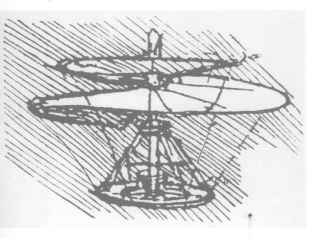

All Nature

During this period in Milan, Leonardo embarked upon his greatest task: to observe, study, draw, and note all aspects of nature to discover the resemblances and patterns within them. He made comparative studies of the legs of a man and a horse, for instance. In his research, he hoped to reveal the patterns and harmonies between all things — to reveal essential truth that explains the world.

▲ Many other artists studied nature; these plants were drawn by the German Albrecht Dürer (1471–1528), an admirer of Leonardo.

▲ Drawing of Cats and a Dragon (c. 1513–15). This sketch by Leonardo shows his belief that humans and animals express emotions in a similar way.

Flying Machines

Since ancient times, people have been speculating about whether humans could fly. From childhood, Leonardo had observed the flight of birds and falling objects such as sycamore seeds. He developed these ideas in a number of notebooks, making sketches that today we recognize as gliders, airplanes, helicopters, and parachutes. To him, human flight was the greatest engineering dream. However, the technology of the time made these concepts impractical. He needed stronger lightweight materials and, above all, the lightweight engines that only became available five centuries later.

To Rome

1506 Under Pope Julius II (1453–1513), work begins on the Basilica of St. Peter's in Rome, designed by Bramante.
1513 Pope Julius II dies and is succeeded by Giovanni de' Medici (1475–1521), who takes the name Leo X.
In September, Leonardo leaves Milan for Rome with Melzi and Salaí.
c. 1514 Leonardo makes plans to drain the Pontine Marshes to rid them of malaria. Bramante dies; Raphael succeeds him as architect of St. Peter's.
1515 Leonardo is accused of being a sorcerer for dissecting bodies and is prevented by the pope from continuing with this activity.

In 1513, Leonardo accepted an invitation to go to Rome. There he spent three years in the service of Giuliano de' Medici (1479–1516), the brother of Pope Leo X and head of the Papal Armies. He lived comfortably in the Palazzo Belvedere in the Vatican, accompanied by Melzi and Salaí, and was given a workshop and German assistants. He devoted himself mainly to his studies, focusing on mechanics, geometry, and optics. He also sketched ancient Roman sculpture and architecture, made plans to drain the Pontine Marshes near Rome, designed pageant costumes, and sketched a plan for a new Medici palace in Florence. But Leonardo was now sixty-one, his eyesight was failing, and he felt tired and unappreciated in Rome.

Rome

For some thirty years, Rome had been building up its reputation as the new capital of the Renaissance. It had attracted many of the best painters in Italy, including Michelangelo and Raphael, as well as the architect Donato Bramante. Bramante was working on the Basilica of St. Peter's. Michelangelo had completed the Sistine Chapel ceiling in 1512, and Raphael was working on a series of frescoes in the Vatican Palace.

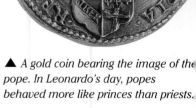

▲ *A gold coin bearing the image of the pope. In Leonardo's day, popes behaved more like princes than priests.*

◀ *Built in 1502, Bramante's Tempietto, inspired by the buildings of the ancient Greeks and Romans, is considered the first pure Renaissance building in Rome.*

▼ *The frescoes of the Stanza dell'Incendio in the Vatican (1514–17) were designed by Raphael and later painted by Giulio Romano (c. 1492–1546). The historical scenes depict earlier Pope Leos — here Pope Leo III — but with Pope Leo X's features.*

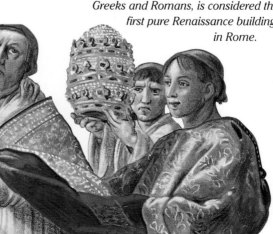

The Popes

The Catholic Church was still recovering from a major crisis called the Great Schism of 1378–1417, a period when there had been two rival popes, one in Avignon in France and one in Rome. Many popes made great efforts to recover their prestige. They were powerful and ruthless politicians as well as great patrons of the arts. This was particularly true of Pope Leo X. Under his papacy, Rome became the center of a new period called the High Renaissance.

Astronomy

Star maps in Leonardo's day were still largely based on the maps of Ptolemy, who had lived some thirteen hundred years before. Characteristically, Leonardo took a different view from that generally held and concluded that Earth is a planetary body floating in space just like any other. His notes and drawings suggest that he may have anticipated the telescope, invented one hundred years later.

◄ *The Greek philosopher Plato (left), as depicted by Raphael in his* School of Athens *(c. 1509–11) in the Vatican. This is said to be a portrait of Leonardo.*

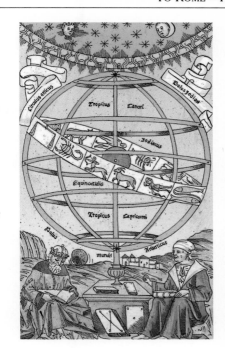

▶ *The Ptolemaic globe, from a book published in Venice in 1496. Scholars sit beneath a schematic model of the heavens, at the center of which is Earth.*

▼ *Leonardo's mysterious* St. John the Baptist *was completed over several years sometime between 1509 and 1517.*

St. John the Baptist

Leonardo appears to have worked on just one painting during this late spell in his life, a picture of *St. John the Baptist*. There are many curious aspects to this work. Normally, St. John was shown as a rough and rugged type, dressed in animal skins. In Leonardo's version, the face is remarkably soft and feminine. St. John's hand gesture, suggesting the path to God, is rather awkward for an artist of such skill as Leonardo. Yet the treatment of the hair and the use of deep shadow and light is typical. In addition, the painting has a silent mystery to it, shared with other Leonardo paintings such as the *Mona Lisa*.

▶ Sagittal and Horizontal Sections of the Head with the Layers of the Head Compared with an Onion *(c. 1489), a cross section of the human head, shows how the eye is connected to the brain.*

Eyesight and Optics

Leonardo thought that observation was the source of artists' skills and the source of knowledge. He was fascinated by the mechanics of sight and studied the function of eye lenses. He also conducted experiments with lenses, glass balls, and mirrors.

Last Days in France

1515 Francis I becomes King of France. He reconquers Milan. In December, Pope Leo X meets Francis I at Bologna. Leonardo may also have met him there.
1516 On the death of his patron Giuliano de' Medici, Leonardo is permitted to accept the invitation of Francis I to leave Italy and live in France. Leonardo moves to Amboise and takes up residence in the Château de Cloux (now Clos Lucé).
1518 Leonardo participates in the festivities for the baptism of the dauphin, the French heir to the throne, and for the wedding of Lorenzo de' Medici (grandson of Lorenzo the Magnificent) to the niece of Francis I.
1519 Leonardo dies on May 2 at Clos Lucé at age sixty-seven.

In 1516, Leonardo accepted an invitation from the new French king Francis I (1494–1547) to be his chief painter, architect, and mechanic at Amboise in France. He traveled there in late 1516, with Francesco Melzi and perhaps Salaí, and took up residence. Among his possessions were the *Mona Lisa* and *St. John the Baptist*, which he finished there. It was a strange kind of exile for the aging Leonardo, but at least he felt appreciated there. The young king spent many hours with him; apparently he deeply admired Leonardo as the greatest expert on painting, sculpture, and architecture and as a sage.

◄ *Portrait of Francis I (c. 1525) by Jean Clouet (c. 1485–1540).*

Life at Clos Lucé

Although sixty-four years old on his arrival in France, Leonardo clearly had not lost all of his great energy and powers. In return for a generous salary, he was kept busy planning buildings for Francis I, designing court entertainments, and generally offering advice. He apparently saw Francis I almost every day.

◄ *Clos Lucé today. It has been converted into a museum in Leonardo's memory.*

▼ *The double spiral staircase at Chambord was possibly designed by Leonardo.*

Francis I

The new French king came to power in 1515 at the age of nineteen. He was a true Renaissance prince, a patron of the arts and scholarship, fired with an enthusiasm for the culture and learning of the Italian city-states. He wanted to bring this culture to France. A number of Italian sculptors, painters, architects, and engineers were already in Amboise when Leonardo arrived there. Francis I's reign, however, was later marred by his long conflict with Charles V, the Holy Roman Emperor and King of Spain.

Palace Designs

In mid-January 1517, Leonardo accompanied the king to Romorantin to plan a new royal residence for the king's mother. He drew up some plans for an extensive palace to be built across the river from prefabricated units, but the project was never completed. Meanwhile, from 1518, Francis I was building a magnificent Renaissance palace for himself at Chambord. It is likely that Leonardo had a hand in this, but records do not show how much.

Visions of the End of the World

During the last few years of his life, Leonardo made a series of powerful drawings of floods. For a man who had sought harmony and tranquility in so much of his work, their brutal force comes as a surprise. They may reflect a growing sense of his own impending death. Perhaps he saw that chaos was a vital part of the order of things — part of the complex harmony of life. In about 1517, Leonardo suffered a stroke and lost the use of his right hand. Afterwards, he spent his days trying to bring order to his thousands of pages of notes — a hopeless task.

▲ *One of Leonardo's Deluge drawings, which he made towards the end of his life — a terrifying vision of destruction.*

▼ *A drawing of Leonardo by an unknown artist made in about 1519.*

The End

On April 23, Leonardo wrote a will, appointing as the executor his friend and follower, Francesco Melzi. Nine days later, he died. Legend claims that he died in the arms of Francis I; whether this is true, the story is a measure of the great esteem in which Leonardo was held by the king.

▲ *Melzi was left with the task of sorting out Leonardo's papers, many of which were later organized into books called codices. This is the* Codex Forster II, *now in London.*

The Legacy of Leonardo

During his lifetime, Leonardo was known mainly as a painter and a sculptor. It was only much later that his notebooks began to emerge, revealing all his scientific work. Now he is thought of as both an artist and a scientist. Leonardo believed that artists held the key to knowledge, and therefore art and science were bound together. Later still, Leonardo was appreciated as a great inventor. Most of all, Leonardo is remembered as the true "Renaissance Man." Through his sheer energy, restless curiosity, and multifaceted gifts, he embodied the spirit of the Renaissance.

◀ *Every day, large crowds gather around the* Mona Lisa. *It is the star painting of the Louvre Museum in Paris, one of the world's biggest art galleries.*

▲ *A portrait of Leonardo from the second edition of Vasari's* Lives of the Most Eminent Painters, Sculptors, and Architects, *published in 1568.*

▼ *Detail of three apostles from the* Last Supper *after its most recent restoration.*

Vasari

It was the painter, architect, and writer Giorgio Vasari (1511–74) who laid the foundations for the appreciation of Renaissance art and architecture. His book *Lives of the Most Eminent Painters, Sculptors, and Architects* was first published in 1550. A second, enlarged edition was published in 1568, with more on Leonardo. Writing within living memory of the artists, he used the reports of people who actually knew them. In about 1557, Vasari was commissioned to paint over Leonardo's ruined *Battle of Anghiari* in the Palazzo Vecchio in Florence.

Fame

Leonardo was famous in his own lifetime, but this fame rested mainly on his paintings, notably the *Last Supper*. However, he completed very few paintings. Many of them have been altered or badly restored, and with some, it is not clear how much of the work was actually done by Leonardo himself. The rarity of his paintings adds to their value, and Leonardo's fame has grown with each new century. Each generation can find something new to see in his work.

Leonardo's Style

The supreme quality of Leonardo's painting and drawing technique and the great poise and beauty of his works placed him in virtually a class of his own during his lifetime. The naturalistic, three-dimensional quality of his painting and his careful observation of the play of light helped to define the new artistic standards of the High Renaissance. Raphael and many others, like Giovanni Bellini, Giorgione, and Correggio (1494–1534), learned a lot from Leonardo's work. Italian Baroque painters also admired Leonardo's work. The painter Michelangelo Merisi da Caravaggio (c. 1571–1610), one of the most famous Baroque painters, made his name through his dramatic use of light and shadow — a technique pioneered by Leonardo.

▶ Young Bacchus *(c. 1595) by Caravaggio. A master of observation, Caravaggio gave his painting an almost photographic quality.*

▶ *The* Codex Leicester, *compiled from c. 1505 to 1515 by Leonardo himself, contains many studies on water, with drawings of currents, waterfalls, and whirlpools. It was bound in the early eighteenth century and later dismembered in 1980. It is now part of the Bill Gates collection in Seattle, Washington.*

Restoration

It is not easy to gain a true impression of what Leonardo's paintings actually looked like when first completed. The color of the *Mona Lisa*, for instance, has faded, especially in her cheeks and lips, and layers of varnish have given the painting a yellowish tinge. These paintings have become so valuable that they are almost impossible to clean and restore. Experts have different opinions about how much can be cleaned away without causing damage. One exception is the *Last Supper*, already much altered and restored when it underwent its most recent restoration. Work began in about 1978 and was completed in 1999.

Codices

Leonardo would have been even more famous if his scientific drawings and notes had been published sooner. Leonardo was partly to blame for not being more organized. Melzi, who inherited the papers, took them back to Italy, but after his death in 1570, bundles of the notes were given away or sold cheaply. Many of them were reordered into subjects in Spain in the seventeenth century, then parts were shipped back to Milan and then to France. There are now essentially ten sets of codices, found in Italy, France, Spain, Great Britain, and the United States.

▶ *For the last two decades of the twentieth century, the* Last Supper *was obscured by scaffolding while a large team of experts worked to clean and restore the painting.*

Glossary

aerial perspective The method of representing objects so as to create an effect of atmosphere. Objects are usually depicted bluer or paler the farther away they are from the picture foreground to give the illusion of depth or far distance.

aerodynamics The scientific study of the forces of moving air, or the forces that act on a moving object.

allegory A story or painting in which characters or figures represent good and bad qualities.

anatomy The study of the organization of the body in separate parts.

apparatus Equipment, machine, or set of instruments that work together for a particular purpose, usually for scientific experiments.

apprenticeship The hiring of a person under agreement to serve, for a specified period of time, a person skilled in a trade, for low wages. In the Renaissance, young boys seeking to become artists received their training by serving as apprentices in the workshops of established artists.

cartography The art of drawing maps or charts.

cartoon A full-size preparatory drawing used to transfer a design to a wall.

cast To shape metal, usually in the creation of a sculpture, by melting it and pouring it into a mold.

city-state A medieval or Renaissance city which, along with its surrounding area, formed an independent state.

classical Term used to describe works of art from ancient Greece or Rome or works that have the same characteristics as the works of ancient Greece or Rome.

codex (pl. Codices) A volume of manuscripts or an original form of an ancient or old, unbound book.

commission The act of appointing someone to do a specified task, or the actual task or duty given to someone under an agreement. Artists in the Renaissance usually signed contracts that stipulated salary and other details pertinent to the work to be produced when they received commissions.

compagnia An Italian term used to describe an association, guild, or confraternity representing a certain trade.

composition The arrangement of the parts of something. Term used to refer to the way in which objects are arranged, usually in a painting or sculpture.

confraternity A brotherhood or association of men united for some worthy purpose, usually a religious charity organization of lay members.

Doge The chief magistrate or official in the former republics of Venice and Genoa.

equestrian A person riding on a horse, or belonging to a rider.

fresco painting A mural painting made by the application of color onto a wall when the top layer of plaster is still wet.

grotesque Having strange or unnatural qualities or proportions.

guild An association representing the different trades or crafts in medieval and Renaissance Europe.

humanism A cultural movement of the fifteenth century based on the study of classical texts, or a system of thought concerned with the needs of man rather than with those of religion.

loggia A gallery or porch, usually with arched openings, open on one or more sides.

optics The science of sight or the study of light.

palazzo Italian word for building or palace.

patron A person or group of people who gives money to a person or group to perform a certain task or for some other worthy purpose.

patron saint A holy man or woman who protects a particular group or community.

perspective The method of representing objects so as to make them appear three-dimensional. The illusion of depth and space or a view extending far into the distance.

Pietà Term used to refer to a work of art that depicts the Virgin Mary holding the dead body of Christ.

pigment Any substance, usually in the form of a fine powder, used as a coloring agent to make paint. A paint or dye.

refectory A large room or hall, usually in a monastery or school, where meals are served.

Renaissance The cultural movement, originating in Italy during the fourteenth century and lasting until the seventeenth century, in which the art, literature, and ideas of ancient Greece were rediscovered and applied to the arts. The artistic style of this period.

Renaissance man A gifted person who seeks to develop all intellectual, physical, and social skills.

restoration A process or act of bringing an object, work of art, or building back to its original state.

Ser An Italian title similar to "sir" in English.

sfumato From the Italian word for "smokey," a term used to describe a painting technique in which colors are blended together to produce a smooth, hazy effect without harsh outlines or shadows.

treatise A literary work, a book or article, in which an author expresses an opinion about a particular subject by examining its principles and treating them with a planned and organized discussion.

vanishing point In drawing, the point in the distance at which parallel lines appear to meet in a perspective drawing.

villa A large estate or residence located in the country or outside a town.

workshop A place where heavy work is carried out, a factory. In the Renaissance, an artist's workshop was run by a master artist who, with the help of various apprentices and assistants, produced works of art. The master artist directed the organization and production of his own workshop.

Index

Index